MW01536770

Devotions From Proverbs

by

Belinda Jo Adams

All devotions were written by
Belinda Jo Adams.

Bible version used is
The King James Version.

Thank you to
Jimmiedean Curriden,
Carol Colley
and Barbara Harris
for editing this work for me.

Previously published at
Silent Word Ministries

© 2006 / 2016 Belinda Jo Adams
All rights reserved: devotions,
photos and cover photo
http://www.belindajo.com

Permission is given by the author
to copy individual devotions
for private or group use, but not
the book as a whole. Please place
author's name on the page.
Thank you.

ISBN-13: 978-1537235486
ISBN-10: 1537235486

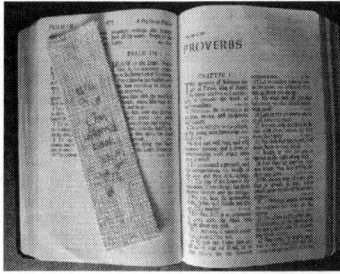

Note from Belinda Jo Adams:

I know in the King James Version, pronouns referring to God and Jesus are not capitalized. I don't know when in our culture that grammar rule was started. In my devotions, I would rather follow the KJV format, for sometimes it gets confusing when there is a capital in the middle of a sentence. However, I decided to follow the rules of our modern day English.

INTRODUCTION

We cannot, in thirty-one days, learn all the writers have for us to discover in Proverbs. It is hard to find only one topic for each chapter because the subjects are mixed throughout the book. I have chosen thirty-one topics and a verse from each chapter to highlight concerning it. Please read the whole chapter as well as the verse I have chosen.

Proverbs teaches godly living by comparing things or ideas. Chapters 1-9 contrasts good and evil. Chapter 10-15 uses the word 'but' to contrasts wisdom and foolishness. Verse 1:7 is the main verse for the book.

"The fear of the LORD is the beginning of knowledge: but fools despise wisdom and instruction."

This fear means reverence or wonder of God. Wisdom is the key word. Chapters 1-9 talk about wisdom 24 times. There are 30 other times wisdom is mentioned throughout the book.

The book of Proverbs points out times that we are to seek wisdom, knowledge, and understanding. Some people have knowledge but not understanding. Some have knowledge without wisdom. It is good to have knowledge and understanding, and then to have wisdom to use what we have learned in our Christian lives. True wisdom comes from God.

Solomon was the wisest man in history. God answered his request for this wisdom. (I Kings 3:5-14) He is famous for his architectural and engineering skills and his ability in leadership. Solomon wrote most of the book with advice to listen to his words of wisdom. He encourages us to heed his words.

A good way to discover all Proverbs has to offer is by reading a chapter each day. It is important for us to learn and to keep on learning all God has for us to know. Ask God for wisdom to understand what Solomon has to tell you.

Honoring Parents

Read: Proverbs Chapter 1

Verse: "My son, hear the instruction of thy father, and forsake not the law of thy mother:" (Proverbs 1:8)

This verse encourages us to honor our parents. How do we honor our parents? Parents want the best for their children. They have a responsibility to teach them to be good. We should obey our parents. We should let them teach us things to help. We can do special things for them to make them happy. It is important to listen to our fathers and be loyal to our mothers. How long? As long as we live.

When children grow up and live good lives it honors parents. Parents are happy to see their children do right when they are young and when they are adults. We can continue honoring our parents when we leave home. We can send letters or visit them. Paying attention to their wisdom is a special way to honor them, also.

Many newspapers publish names of couples celebrating their fiftieth wedding anniversary. Sometimes their children give them a party to celebrate. But, why wait until they are old to honor them? We can do little things for them now.

"Honor thy father and thy mother: that thy days may be long upon the land which the Lord thy God giveth thee." (Exodus 20:12)

God promises us a longer life if we honor our parents. Think today how you can honor your parents and make them happy. Tell your parents you love them. Then show you love them by doing something special for them.

Related Proverbs verses: 3:1-2; 4:10; 4:20-22; 6:20; 20:20; 23:19 & 22

Thought: Honor your parents today.

Hear the instruction of thy father, and forsake not the law of thy mother.

Wisdom and Understanding

Read: Proverbs Chapter 2

Verse: "Discretion shall preserve thee, understanding shall keep thee: To deliver thee from the way of the evil man, from the man that speaketh froward things;" (Proverbs 2:11-12)

Discretion means to choose what to do. God gives wisdom and understanding to choose right. He tells us to get wisdom and understanding. When we do, we will be able to walk in the right way. Then people will not lead us wrong. We will know what God wants and can resist the devil.

> Joseph worked for Potiphar. Potiphar's wife noticed how nice Joseph was. She decided she wanted him to be with her. While her husband was gone she tried to tempt Joseph to come into her bedroom. Joseph used discretion and ran away from the evil woman. (Genesis 39:7-12)

"Submit yourselves therefore to God. Resist the devil, and he will flee from you. Draw nigh unto God, and he will draw nigh unto you." (James 4:7-8a)

James was written many years after Joseph, but Joseph knew the importance of doing right, and he ran away from sin.

Is it hard to say "no" to sin? Do you want to join when friends do wrong so they will not make fun of you? Maybe you worry they will not accept you. God wants you to say 'no' to sin and not worry about what people think. True friends will not want you to do wrong. When you read the Bible God shows you what he wants you to know, and the right way to live. Then you can choose to do right and not sin. As you do what God wants then God gives you strength to choose right.

Related Proverbs verses: 1:2; 2:2; 3:13; 4:7; 5:1

Thought: Run away from sin.

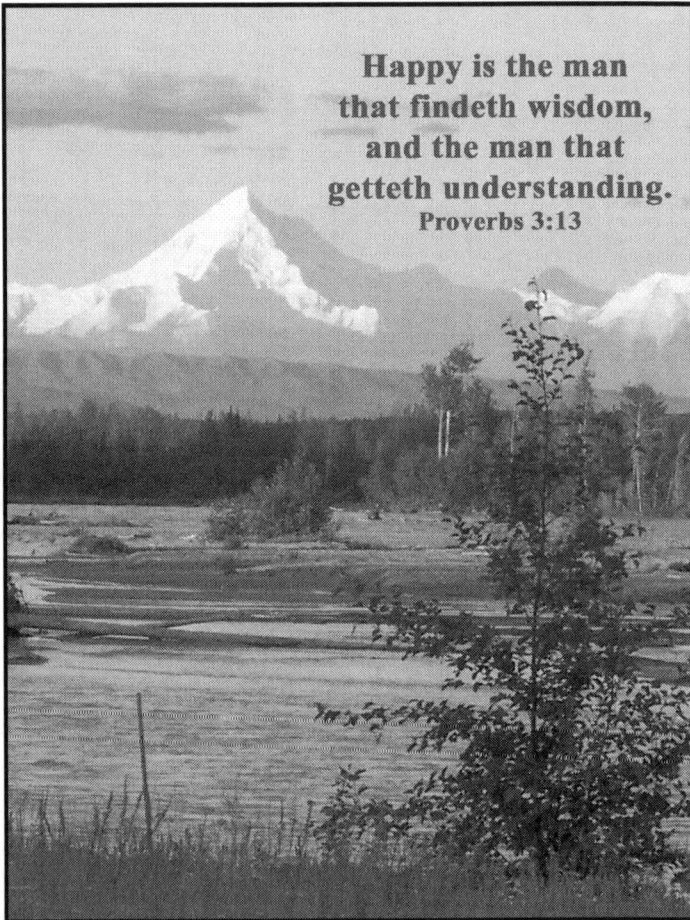

Happy is the man that findeth wisdom, and the man that getteth understanding.
Proverbs 3:13

Giving to God

Read: Proverbs Chapter 3

Verse: "Honour the LORD with thy substance, and with the firstfruits of all thine increase:" (Proverbs 3:9)

This verse teaches to honor God by giving to Him offerings before we do anything else with our money. It is important to remember to give money to God's work before other needs. God will bless what we keep by making it buy more.

Sometimes people say, "I don't want to go to church. All that preacher wants is money." Some preachers seem to talk about nothing else, but any organization needs money to stay operating. The church has to pay rent, electric and water just like we have to pay our own rent, electric, and water. People enjoy the nice buildings, but it seems no one wants to pay for the use of them. If a church is to help the community and missionaries, it has to have money.

The Old Testament law commands that a tithe, one-tenth, of our income, be given back to God. Abraham gave tithes of all he had. (Genesis 14:18-20) Abraham gave a tithe before the Old Testament law was given. He knew it was important.

The New Testament tells us in II Corinthians 9:7b, "... for God loveth a cheerful giver". God is concerned why we give more than what we give. If we give with a bad attitude God cannot bless it. It is better to give with a good attitude and receive God's blessings on our lives. We should never give to get praise from others.

Give to God and He will give to you.

Walk in the Right Way

Read: Proverbs Chapter 4

Verse: "Enter not into the path of the wicked, and go not in the way of evil men. Avoid it, pass not by it, turn from it, and pass away." (Proverbs 4:14-15)

God does not want us to fellowship with sinners. God warns Christians to stay away from wicked places and evil people. Paul warns against this in II Corinthians 6:17a "Wherefore come out from among them, and be ye separate, saith the Lord, and touch not the unclean thing; ..."

George Williams lived in England during the 1800's. Many men left their farms to work in factories in town. In 1841 George left his family farm to work at a store. The many temptations to sin bothered him. Working many hours he did not have much time alone for Bible study. He soon found several other men who believed in God. They made opportunities to study the Bible and have prayer together which helped them resist temptations to sin. Others joined the group of men and the Young Men's Christian Association (YMCA) began June 6, 1844.

Are you around people at home, school, or your job who are not Christians? Are you tempted to join in with their sinning? Do you find it hard to find time to read your Bible? Start with five minutes a day to read a few verses and pray. Share special verses God shows you with family or friends. You will be surprised how soon you will be having a longer time with God daily and wanting to be around people who serve Him.

Related Proverbs verses: 2:10-20

Thought: To walk in the right way – Read your Bible and pray.

With This Ring

Read: Proverbs Chapter 5

Verse: "Let thy fountain be blessed: and rejoice with the wife of thy youth." (Proverbs 5:18)

In verses 15-21, Solomon is teaching his son to remain faithful to his wife that he married when he was young. He tells his son that when he marries a woman he should stay married to her until he or she dies. This is the way to be happy.

Jesus' first miracle was performed at a wedding. He said "Wherefore they are no more twain, but one flesh. What therefore God hath joined together, let no man put asunder" (Matthew 19:6).

This means that a married couple are no longer two people, but one in God's sight. There is something special about the beauty of a couple who have been married many years and their lives show they care for each other. It should be the goal of the man and woman from their wedding day to continue loving each other. God never meant for people to divorce. He means for married people to make peace when they have problems and ask God to bless their marriage so they can stay married.

> Have you ever glued two things together then tried to pull them apart later? They never come apart to stay the same as when they were before they were glued together.

Maybe your marriage is having trouble. You need to try to keep it together by prayer and working together. Ask God to help you make it your goal to give 100% to your partner by making memories that will make your life together the best you will ever know. This way you can fulfill a life of love, faithfulness, and companionship.

Related Proverbs verses: 15:17; 17:1

What God has joined together, let no man separate.

Thought: God wants you to have a happy marriage.

Gossip Hurts

Read: Proverbs Chapter 6

Verse: "These six things doth the Lord hate: yea, seven are an abomination unto him: A proud look, a lying tongue, and hands that shed innocent blood, An heart that deviseth wicked imaginations, feet that be swift in running to mischief, A false witness that speaketh lies, and he that soweth discord among brethern." (Proverbs 6:16-19)

> A proud look is when a person thinks he is better than other people. God created all people equal. We need to treat all people the same and not mock people who are different. A lying tongue does not make God happy. God will bless if you are honest with others. Hands that shed innocent blood is when someone kills someone else. A heart that deviseth wicked imaginations is thinking bad thoughts. Feet that be swift in running to mischief is not behaving. A false witness is when a person lies about another person. He that soweth discord among brethren can be gossiping and causing trouble among people.

Paul warns us in Ephesians 4:30-32 not to grieve the Holy Spirit and lists examples. One of these is by evil speaking. When we find out something bad that happened to someone else, we should not tell others. The story usually changes from person to person and turns to gossip. And, the story may not have been true in the beginning.

When someone hurts us we should not be angry, but love and forgive them. We should not talk to others about the problem. It is right that we go to the person and make peace. Satan wants friends to become enemies because of gossip. We ought not to gossip about people. It can only hurt and does not please God.

Related Proverbs verses: 11:13; 12:6; 17:9; 18:8; 26:20

Thought: Ask God to help you not gossip.

"And grieve not the holy Spirit of God,

whereby ye are sealed unto the day of

redemption. Let all bitterness, and wrath,

and anger, and clamour, and evil speaking,

be put away from you, with all malice:

And be ye kind one to another,

tenderhearted, forgiving one another,

even as God for Christ's sake

hath forgiven you."

Ephesians 4:30-32

Bible Memory

Read: Proverbs Chapter 7

"My son, keep my words, and lay up my commandments with thee." (Proverbs 7:1)

Verses 1-4 and verses 24-25 of this chapter warn to keep and obey God's Word to fight Satan trying to tempt us. We need to keep our minds on God's Word and what He wants in our lives. Then we will know what sin is so we can stay away from it and stay pure.

> "This book will keep you away from sin and sin will keep you away from this Book." This is a quote I heard when I was a teenager. It has been written in each Bible I have owned and given to others since then.

The quote is so true. When we have our minds on what the Bible says, then we will be able to stay away from sin. If we take time to study and memorize God's commandments, then try to obey them by living right, God will bless our lives. God will help us remember those commandments as good rules to follow and we will have a better life.

Psalm 119:11, written by King David, tells us to hide God's Word in our hearts that we might not sin against God. The Bible considers the heart as the place of understanding. These verses in Chapter seven, written by Solomon, King David's son, reinforces that thought to his son more than three thousand years ago and to us today!

Related Proverbs verses: 4:1; 8:10;19:20

Thought: The Bible will keep you away from sin and sin will keep you away from the Bible.

The Riches of Wisdom

Read: Proverbs Chapter 8

Verse: "For wisdom is better than rubies; and all the things that may be desired are not to be compared to it." (Proverbs 8:11)

These verses talk about wisdom being better than gold, silver, or rubies. Wisdom dwelled with God before anything was created (see verses 22-30) God tells people to seek wisdom for a life of happiness. Wise people will hate sin and stay away from its evil works.

> During the 1840's in the United States was the famous Gold Rush. Men left home and loved ones behind with the promise of a brighter, richer future. They traveled great distances over dangerous oceans, mountains, and deserts in hope to get great riches and honor. Many lost their lives in this search. Some found gold only to have their riches vanish by cheaters and thieves seeking an easier way to become wealthy. Only few became rich and we wonder if they had the joy they hoped to get.

"If any of you lack wisdom, let him ask of God, that giveth to all men liberally, and upbraideth not; and it shall be given him." (James 1:5)

Upbraideth means to scold. God will not scold us for asking for wisdom. He will give us what we ask for and that wisdom will be more valuable than all the riches in the world!

Money might make you forget God. God wants you to serve Him more than you want to be rich. Pray for God's wisdom to live your life as He wants and to use what money He gives you in the right way.

Related Proverbs verses: 1:7; 2:6; 3:13; 16:16

The Knowledge of The Holy

Read: Proverbs Chapter 9

Verse: "The fear of the Lord is the beginning of wisdom: and the knowledge of the holy is understanding." (Proverbs 9:10)

The fear of the Lord means to trust God with a faithful trust and to hate evil. Job tells us in Job 28:28 that "the fear of the Lord, that is wisdom ...".

One way we can know more about God is to study His personality. Just like we have a personality, God does, too. Sometimes our personality changes. God's personality never changes. God is the same past, present, and future.

God is Spiritual (holy), Infinite (endless), Eternal (endless), Freedom, Always same, Perfect, Just (fair), Love, Truth, Mercy, Grace (forgives us when we do not deserve forgiving), Omnipotence (All powerful), Omnipresence (All present), and Omniscience (All knowing) A study of each of these personalities gives new understanding of God and His love for people.

Many things happen in life that we may not understand, but as Christians we should love God and continue to trust Him to work in our lives. Sometimes, it is hard to understand some of the Bible verses. Some are easy, but some are hard to understand. Nobody understands all the Bible. By faith we have to trust God and believe the verses that are hard to understand.

If you wish for a better understanding of the Word of God and why things happen in life, start reading the Bible! When you read the Bible, God can speak to your heart and mind. God helps you understand more and gives you peace for the things you do not understand.

Related Proverbs verses: 2:3-6; 18:15;19:2; 23:12

Thought: To know God is to love Him.

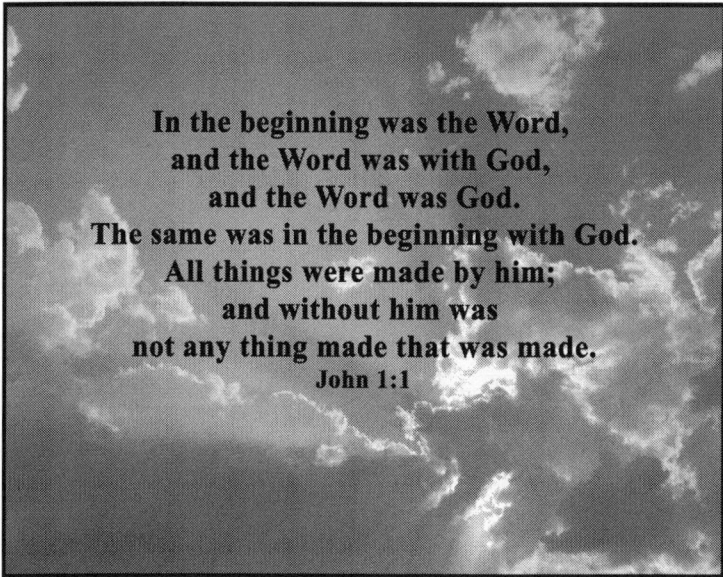

> In the beginning was the Word,
> and the Word was with God,
> and the Word was God.
> The same was in the beginning with God.
> All things were made by him;
> and without him was
> not any thing made that was made.
> **John 1:1**

GOD

IS

Precious Memories

Read: Proverbs Chapter 10

Verse: "The memory of the just is blessed: but the name of the wicked shall rot." (Proverbs 10:7)

Can you think of a person you know who did nice things for other people? Do you have good things to say about them? When a person lives to help others, then people remember that person with good thoughts.

My husband's great-grandmother had good things to say about other people. When she was in a conversation where her friends criticized someone, she said something positive about that person. She felt there was something good about each person. Her grandchildren remember her for that good attitude.

We should be careful of what we say. Just because we see a person do wrong is no reason to run and tell others about it. We should pray for them and seek the right time to encourage them to do better.

When we have the love of God in our hearts, we should not talk about other people's faults just as they should not talk about ours. Then we can all get along with others and be doing God's business of witnessing to people.   (charity = love)

"And above all things have fervent charity among yourselves: for charity shall cover the multitude of sins." (1 Peter 4:8)

Show love to your brothers and sisters in Christ and others so when you are in Heaven they will have good memories of you.

Related Proverbs verses: 10:12; 17:9; 22:1

Soul Winning

Read: Proverbs Chapter 11

Verse: "The fruit of the righteous is a tree of life; and he that winneth souls is wise." (Proverbs 11:30)

God wants Christians to be busy winning other people to Jesus. God wants all people to be saved. He does not use angels to do this great job. Before he returned to Heaven, he instructed his disciples to win others. Jesus said He would be with them as they obeyed him.

"Go ye therefore, and teach all nations, baptizing them in the name of the Father, and of the Son, and of the Holy Ghost: Teaching them to observe all things whatsoever I have commanded you: and, lo, I am with you alway, even unto the end of the world. Amen." (Matthew 28:19-20)

Some people can witness easy. Others find it hard to witness because they are shy, but Jesus can help us overcome shyness. There are ways we can witness if we don't know what to say. As we go about our daily lives we can be a witness to others by the way we live. When God opens a way for us to present the story of Jesus to them, He will give us courage to do it. Then we may have a chance to win a soul to Jesus.

We can invite people to come to church to have the gospel presented to them as the pastor preaches. Giving out tracts is a good way to witness. We can give them to people or leave them in places so people can find them. We can place a tract in each envelope when we pay bills and write letters to friends.

Related Proverbs verses: 22:19-21

Truthfulness

Read: Proverbs Chapter 12

Verse: "He that speaketh truth sheweth forth righteousness: but a false witness deceit. (Proverbs 12:17)

> The poet read the poem to the group. He wanted the other writers to tell him how good it was. But, the poem was not good. The other writers looked at each other, then several writers tried to give advice on how to improve his work. The young man became upset. He did not understand that true friends help each other with advice to help them improve.
> When one person told him it was good just the way it was, he thanked him and took his treasure home.

When we pay attention to good advice it can help us become a better person. People need to know they can trust us to tell them the truth and not lie to them.

Sometimes it is not easy to know the truth. Jesus knew where lies come from. Satan tempts people to be deceitful.

"Ye are of your father the devil, and the lusts of your father ye will do. He was a murderer from the beginning, and abode not in the truth, because there is no truth in him. When he speaketh a lie, he speaketh of his own: for he is a liar, and the father of it." (John 8:44)

We should make it our goal to be truthful with people so we can help them. Liars hurt themselves and other people with their lies. It is better to be truthful than to be deceitful. But, sometimes, even the truth can hurt, so be careful.

Related Proverbs verses: 17:4

Goal Accomplished!

Read: Proverbs Chapter 13

Verse: "The desire accomplished is sweet to the soul: ..." (Proverbs 13: 19)

It makes us happy to do something we have been wanting to do. It is good to set goals and then seek to do things that we desire.

> The Olympic games have been going on for many centuries. The participants train to do their very best. They set aside personal desires and time with their family and friends. Their goal is to win the medal. As they play in games with the crowd cheering them on, they give their all for the sport. If that same person had sat home and never tried they would not have that sweet moment of success.

"Wherefore seeing we also are compassed about with so great a cloud of witnesses, let us lay aside every weight, and the sin which doth so easily beset us, and let us run with patience the race that is set before us," (Hebrews 12:1)

Here, Paul tells us that Christians are in a race in service to God. Maybe we have to set aside personal desires and not join in with our friends to reach a goal God wants for us to accomplish.

"Looking unto Jesus the author and finisher of our faith; ..." (Hebrews 12:2)

Jesus is our guide and besides the crowns we win, His "well done" will be our trophy. If we sit and do nothing we will never see our goals completed.

We need to let God help us set goals in our lives each day so we don't get caught in Satan's trick of being lazy. Then we need to get up and do something about those goals. A list of things to do on a table will only collect dust. It needs to collect pencil lines as we mark off each accomplished goal.

Related Proverbs verses: 29:18

Thought:

Set a goal today.

Then, with God's help, do it!

Choosing a Good Church

Read: Proverbs Chapter 14

Verse: "The simple believeth every word: but the prudent man looketh well to his going." (Proverbs 14:15)

Solomon is teaching to be wise when choosing people to trust. Some people are good at telling lies and making people believe them. Pray for wisdom from God when deciding who to believe and which church to join.

Some religious leaders are included in Solomon's warning. There have been many times where a man or woman claimed to be a prophet of God. People followed them, sometimes to their death. They changed the words of the Bible to say what they wanted it to say.

"Howbeit in vain do they worship me, teaching for doctrine the commandments of men." (Mark 7:7)

Good people give their time and money to these preachers. Later they find out the truth and are disappointed.

When we do not study the Bible for ourselves we take a chance of following a leader who can lead us away from the truth of God's Word.

"Study to shew thyself approved unto God, a workman that needeth not to be ashamed, rightly dividing the word of truth." (II Timothy 2:15)

Pray for God to lead you to the church and pastor to teach you right things to do from God's will. As you seek the right church and pastor, try asking yourself these questions: Do the members of the church live as Jesus wants? Does the pastor proclaim salvation by grace through faith, not by works? Good pastors will always point you to Jesus and not to themselves.

Related Proverbs verses: 4:2; 30:5 & 6

Trust Your Pastor's Teaching

Read: Proverbs Chapter 15

Verse: "He that refuseth instruction despiseth his own soul: but he that heareth reproof getteth understanding." (Proverbs: 15:32)

God has given preachers to lead His people in the right way. Preachers encourage the members of their churches to live right and serve God. Sometimes this includes reminding us what sin is.

Some people think going to church, being baptized, giving to help others, or doing volunteer work at the church and for the community is all they need to do. They think they can do good things and go to Heaven. When preachers remind them of their sin, they become full of pride and refuse to listen.

If we are not obeying God with clean lives then we are not right with Him and all the special things we do will not help. Salvation is a free gift. We do not have to work for it. When we accept Jesus as Savior, we have the promise of Heaven. Then we need to live right to honor God and receive His blessings. But, when our pastor preaches and the Holy Spirit reminds us of a sin we need to confess as we pay attention and obey. We can trust what the Bible teaches.

The last devotion encouraged us to pray and choose the right church and pastor. Now we should pay attention to our pastor as he leads us to serve God.

As you committed your life to God and trusted Him to lead you to the right church, you can depend on God to help you learn from the man of God, your pastor, as he teaches you from God's Word, the Bible.

Related Proverbs verses: 13:18; 15:12 & 32

That Does Not Compute

Read: Proverbs Chapter 16

Verse: "Commit thy works unto the Lord, and thy thoughts shall be established." (Proverbs 16:3)

To commit is to do something on purpose. That means a person chooses to do something. This verse tells us to commit our works unto the Lord. When we walk with the Lord, He promises our thoughts will stay right. We will not have to worry about having wrong thoughts if we keep our minds on Him.

Computers can be wonderful. They accomplish many different jobs and make our life lives easier. They seem to think for themselves! The computer can only do what it is told. What comes out must first go into its memory. Sometimes wrong things come out because wrong things were put in. "garbage in – garbage out"

"And the peace of God, which passeth all understanding, shall keep your hearts and minds through Christ Jesus." (Philippians 4:7)
The thought life is a hard part of living the Christian life. Verse 8, of the same chapter, tells us that if anything is true, honest, just, pure, lovely, of good report, be of any virtue, or of any praise; to think on those things. Just as the computer only puts out what is put in, we should guard what is put into our minds.
God knows our thoughts. We need to keep a clean mind as we live right for Him. If we think right then what we say and do will be right.

Related Proverbs verses: 12:5; 21:2; 23:7

A Merry Heart

Read: Proverbs Chapter 17

Verse: "A merry heart doeth good like a medicine: ..."
(Proverbs 17:22)

Solomon knew that a good laugh can help a person feel better. He encourages us to enjoy life.

> Some doctors say if people laugh they will get well faster. There is a clinic where they have TVs for patients to watch while waiting for the doctor. All they show are funny shows. They say this is good for their patients.

The merry heart does not have to sing but usually is happy enough to at least feel like it. The Psalms were written as songs. David wrote many of them. He had a rough life, but he could still sing. He said in Psalm 40:3, "And he hath put a new song in my mouth, even praise unto our God: many shall see it, and fear, and shall trust in the Lord".
The Bible talks about singing about 280 times!
"Let the word of Christ dwell in you richly in all wisdom; teaching and admonishing one another in psalms and hymns and spiritual songs, singing with grace in your hearts to the Lord." (Colossians 3:16)
A nice way to end devotion time is with a song. If you think you can't sing, then read it. Throughout the day the words to that song may come to mind and give comfort or encouragement.

Related Proverbs verse: 29:6

Thought: Satan does not like for Christians to sing.

So ... Sing!

True Friends

Read: Proverbs Chapter 18

Verse: "A man that hath friends must shew himself friendly: and there is a friend that sticketh closer than a brother." (Proverbs 18:24)

      To have friends, we must be friendly. Some people sit around and complain because they do not have friends, but never smile or try to help others. We need to encourage others either by speaking to them or, at least giving them a smile. It seems a little selfish to want others to smile or speak to us first.

      During a lifetime people only have a few true, close friends. We may have many friends during our lives, but only a few will stand by our side through hard times as well as good times. We should try to make friends who will help encourage us.

      Having many friends does not mean that we will always have happiness, even though some of them can be encouraging and helpful. Sometimes friends can take us away from serving God.

      "Be not deceived: evil communications corrupt good manners" (I Corinthians 15:33)

      Paul warns that when we are with people who are not doing right and serving God, then we will not want to serve God and do right.

      Children and adults have a problem with wanting to do whatever makes others happy even though it is wrong. This is called peer pressure. In I Peter 2:9, Peter says we are a peculiar (odd) people. It is hard to stand alone, but true friends will not let us stand alone.

      True friends will support us when we choose to do right, but will also correct us when we do wrong.

Wrong friends can lead us away from God. We need to leave bad friends and love our good Christian friends.

Related Proverbs verses: 22:24-25; 27:6

Thought: Choose your friends wisely.

To have friends,

one must be friendly.

Helping the Poor

Read: Proverbs Chapter 19

Verse: "He that hath pity upon the poor lendeth unto the Lord; and that which he hath given will he pay him again." (Proverbs 19:17)

This verse encourages us to help people in need. It tells that God will bless what is done for others. God rewards the person who gives to poor and needy people.

> Jane Addams lived from 1860 - 1935. She had a great concern for poor people, especially women. In 1889 Jane Addams and Ellen Gates Starr established a social settlement in Chicago called Hull House. They helped many needy women during the years.

Many verses in Proverbs warn against laziness and tells people who would be lazy they would also be poor. As Christians, we should not approve of a lazy attitude. Many people are poor because of hard times. Those people need help. There are many programs that help people in need. We should pray that God will lead us to one we can support or do things on our own as God leads. We cannot give more to God than He gives back to us. As we help the needy, God will help us.

"For ye know the grace of our Lord Jesus Christ, that, though he was rich, yet for your sakes he became poor, that ye through his poverty might be rich." (II Corinthians 8:9)

Jesus left riches of Heaven to be born in a stable and grow up as a carpenter's son. He knew what it was like to be poor.

Related Proverbs verses: 14:31; 17:5; 21:13; 22:9; 28:27; 29:7; 31:20

Shining Lights

Read: Proverbs Chapter 20

Verse: "The spirit of man is the candle of the LORD, ..." (Proverbs 20:27)

Christians are to be candles of the Lord. We are to live our lives in such a way as to warn others of the dangers of continuing in sin.

Jesus said, "Let your light so shine before men, that they may see your good works, and glorify your Father which is in heaven" (Matthew 5:16).

Some people say, "I have Christ as my Savior and am going to Heaven so it doesn't matter how I live." Yes, it does! God wants us to live so people can see Jesus through us.

"That ye may be blameless and harmless, the sons of God, without rebuke, in the midst of a crooked and perverse nation, among whom ye shine as lights in the world;" (Philippians 2:15)

Cape Hatteras is on the easternmost point of a line of islands off the coast of North Carolina. That area is known as the 'graveyard of the Atlantic' because of bad storms and dangerous rocks. These dangers have caused many ships to sink off that coast. Since 1798 lighthouses have been built from Cape Hatteras to Cape Lookout to warn sailors of these dangers. The lighthouse keeper has a responsibility of making sure the light stays burning.

Children in Sunday school sing *This little light of mine, I'm going to let it shine!* We should let our light shine also, so others will come to Christ by our witness.

We can let Jesus shine through us by doing things right and avoiding sin. This way we will be a good witness to others.

Just as the lighthouse keeper makes sure the light is in its best condition, make sure your light (life) shines for Jesus!

Related Proverbs verses: 4:18; 13:9

Thought: Let your life witness for Jesus

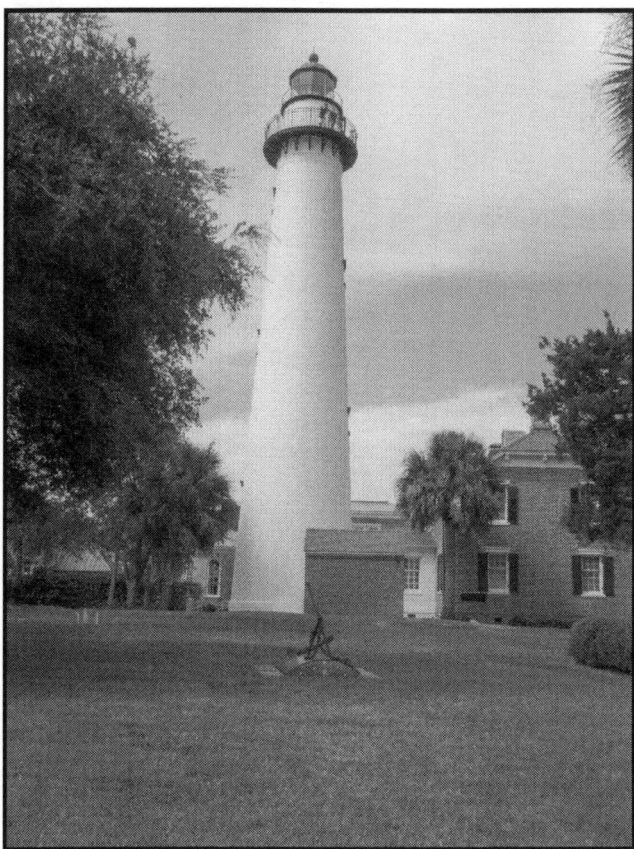

Trust God for Safety

Read: Proverbs Chapter 21

Verse: "The horse is prepared against the day of battle: but safety is of the LORD." (Proverbs 21:31)

No matter how prepared we are against bad things happening in our lives, only God can truly protect us from harm. His guardian angels watch over us and protect us as we go through life.
"The angel of the LORD encampeth round about them that fear him, and delivereth them." (Psalms 34:7)

> The army lined up for battle against another nation's army. The commander of the army took a few moments alone to ask God's blessing on the battle. He asked God's protection for his people. He knew they were prepared for the battle but only God could give safety.

Not only do we trust God in wars, but in our daily lives. The news is full of stories about people being robbed or killed. Car and plane wrecks happen daily. If we pay too much attention to all that is happening in the world, we may become scared to leave home. We need to use common sense and do things to protect ourselves and our families. At the same time, we should pray and ask God for His protection.
Sometimes bad things happen to good people, but remember, God is still in control. Sometimes He lets things happen to us that we don't understand, but God will give us peace to help through those problems.
"And we know that all things work together for good to them that love God, to them who are the called according to his purpose." (Romans 8:28)

Related Verses:11:8; 12:21; 18:10; 30:5

A Good Name

Read: Proverbs Chapter 22

Verse: "A Good name is rather to be chosen than great riches, and loving favour rather than silver and gold." (Proverbs 22:1)

It is better to have a good name than great riches. Sometimes riches come with Satan's temptation not to accept God or not serve Him the way you did before the riches. But, a good name is an honor to God.

What comes to mind when you hear the name Ruth, Moses, Joseph, Esther, Daniel, or Paul in the Bible. They were a few of the people who served God and did right. When troubles came into their lives they still served God and were a witness to others around them. Joseph, and Esther, each saved their nation from destruction because of their trust in God. Daniel in the Old Testament and Paul in the New Testament trusted God when their lives were in danger. They also were a good testimony to their friends and neighbors. Ruth obeyed her elders and became the wife of a famous man, and later, Jesus was born from their lineage.

A good testimony is needed among Christians. The world is looking at our lives to see if we are really living the way a Christian should. If we do not do right, then other people will not want anything to do with church or God. But, if we keep our word, stay away from sin, and live for Jesus, people will see Christ. Then, we will have a good name (testimony) as believers in Jesus.

Related Proverbs verses: 11:27; 31:30-31

Child Rearing

Read: Proverbs 23

Verse: "Withhold not correction from the child: for if thou beatest him with the rod, he shall not die. Thou shalt beat him with the rod, and shalt deliver his soul from hell." (Proverbs 23:13-14)

Some people use these verses to say God says to beat their children. God does not want parents to beat their children. If God did, He would punish us daily for our failures. Some children are too scared to move because of fear of their parents. But, some parents are embarrassed in public because of children who know they can get away with anything.

Discipline is training to help strengthen. It can include various means so order can be upheld. If we set rules for our children and have a punishment equal to the misbehavior, then we can keep order. Sometimes that means taking away privileges or other means to teach them to obey. This may include spanking, but never does it mean to beat children.

"Fathers, provoke not your children to anger, lest they be discouraged." (Colossians 3:21)

When we set rules for our children, we should not make them so high they cannot reach them. We need to understand what is best for each child at each age as he grows up. We also need to be a good example for our children.

If we, like King David from the Bible, will say, "Come, ye children, hearken unto me: I will teach you the fear of the Lord" (Psalm 34:11) then, teach our children to honor and trust God, we can trust Proverbs 22:6 which says, "Train up a child in the way he should go: and when he is old, he will not depart from it".

Related Proverbs verses: 13:24;19:18; 23:26; 29:15

Thought: Train your child to follow God.

The American Dream

Read: Proverbs Chapter 24

Verse: "Through wisdom is an house builded; and by understanding it is established: And by knowledge shall the chambers be filled with all precious and pleasant riches." (Proverbs 24:3-4)

Solomon says that the wise person will do well to follow God's plan for a happy home. Proverbs teaches that wisdom, understanding, and knowledge are the key requirements for a happy home. Ephesians 5:21-25 and Colossians 3:17-23 are good verses to read on the home.

People leave other countries to come to America for the 'American Dream'. They are looking for a home of their own. Real estate agents, banks, and home improvement centers make money from people who are looking for their perfect home. But, the house is not the home; the family inside the house is the home.

"Nethertheless let every one of you in particular so love his wife even as himself; and the wife see that she reverence her husband." (Ephesians 5:33)

If a husband loves his wife as much as he loves himself, it will truly be easy for the wife to honor his wishes in their life and follow his lead. If parents teach children as God would have them and not make them discouraged, then children will want to please their parents by obeying them.

We should love our wife or husband as much as we love ourselves. We should take time to read our Bible and pray with our family. If we teach our children how to do right by our example, then doing these things, we can truly have the real 'American Dream' of a happy home!

Related Proverbs verses: 11:29; 14:1; 15:6; 17:1

Thought: Let God help you have a happy home.

Praise God for the house
He gives to you
for your family to live in.

Home Sweet Home

A Time of Sorrow

Read: Proverbs 25

Verse: "As he that taketh away a garment in cold weather, and as vinegar upon nitre, so is he that singeth songs to an heavy heart." (Proverbs 25: 20)

When someone is mourning the death of a friend or relative, friends often say happy things or quote Bible verses to help them feel better. This verse says not to sing to a sad heart. When people do these things, it is like taking away a person's coat when it is wintertime or pouring vinegar into a sore.

> Our bodies and minds are closely connected in more ways than one. When we are sad our body reacts to our feelings. During sad times people try to get others to eat and keep up their strength, but it is good not to eat as much and let the digestive system rest.

We need to let the person with sorrow know we are thinking about them and praying for them. We need to give them encouragement, but people have to deal with their own feelings. We cannot know exactly how another person feels about anything. Some things we say may only make the person more upset. Sometimes our presence is more important than words. Our presence and encouragement gives people in sorrow a chance to share their feelings if they want to. We can pray for them, but only God can comfort their hearts and give them peace to enjoy life again.

"Blessed be God, even the Father of our Lord Jesus Christ, the Father of mercies, and the God of all comfort;" (II Corinthians 1:3)

Related Proverbs verses: 12:25; 14:10

Laziness

Read: Proverbs Chapter 26

Verse: "As the door turneth upon his hinges, so doth the slothful upon his bed." (Proverbs 26:14)

Much of this chapter is about the foolish or lazy person. Proverbs warns many times about working for what we need. We cannot sit around and do nothing and still have our needs given to us. We should work for what we get.

There is a story from Aesop's Fables called *The Ant and the Grasshopper*. The ants worked all summer gathering food. The grasshopper did nothing but sing. When winter came the grasshopper went to the ants begging for food. They asked him why he did not have any. He explained he was too busy singing during the summer to gather food. They did not share with him.

"For even when we were with you, this we commanded you, that if any would not work, neither should he eat." (II Thessalonians 3:10)

The first people to settle in the Jamestown Colony went by this rule. The people who were used to being waited on by servants while in England thought they should have this service now, also. They soon learned that each person had to do his own job to help the new colony survive.

It is a lot easier to stay in bed when the alarm rings, but we will not get much accomplished that way. We need to do our jobs so we do not have to beg when we need things. God will bless us as we work and earn what we need in life.

Related Proverbs verses: 10:26; 15:19; 22:13

Will We Be Alive Tomorrow?

Read: Proverbs Chapter 27

Verse: "Boast not thyself of to morrow; for thou knowest not what a day may bring forth."
(Proverbs 27:1)

This verse warns not to brag about what we will do tomorrow because we do not know if we will be alive then. People throughout time have lived how they wanted to live, then at a bad time called upon God. God will save a person when they ask Him, even on a deathbed, but why wait? We can have a lifetime of days to serve God by accepting Him and living for Him instead of waiting until life seems finished.

The sinking of the Titanic was one of history's greatest ship wrecks. Approximately 2,200 people of the Titanic traveled on the safest and largest ship at that time. The passengers traveled across the Atlantic Ocean in safety until disaster happened. During the night of April 14, 1912 the ship hit an iceberg. Two and a half hours later more than 1,500 people died. Many of them, during their last minutes, called upon God for mercy.

We do not have to wait until an accident or sickness strikes to call upon God. Jesus came, died, and rose again so we can have everlasting life. All we have to do is believe, repent of our sins, and accept Jesus.
(see: John 3:16 & I Corinthians 15:1-4)
"... behold, now is the accepted time; behold, now is the day of salvation." (II Corinthians 6:2b)

Related Proverbs verse: 8:35

Fearing God

Read: Proverbs Chapter 28

Verse: "Happy is the man that feareth alway: but he that hardenth his heart shall fall into mischief." (Proverbs 28:14)

      The main verse for the whole book of Proverbs is, "The fear of the LORD is the beginning of knowledge:" (Proverbs 1:7)
      This message is repeated in Proverbs 9:10, Psalm 111:10 and Job 28:28. This fear means honor or wonder of God. Fear is the respect for laws.

Sometimes parents tell their children to do something and when the child does not obey they start counting to three to give that child time to obey. This lets the child know that he does not have to obey at first. Maybe she still has two chances! When parents expect their children to obey when first told, the children have a 'fear' of their parents. Not a scary fear, but a trusting fear to know their parents care that they do right.

      "And we know that all things work together for good to them that love God, to them who are the called according to his purpose." (Romans 8:28)
      God has a plan for us and wants to guide our lives in that plan. Will we trust God to lead?
      As we read the Bible and find verses of God's love, guidance, and protection we should praise God from whom all these blessing flow!

Related Proverbs verses: 3:7; 10:27; 14:26; 15:16

An Assassin's Anger

Read: Proverbs 29

Verse: "An angry man stirreth up strife, and a furious man aboundeth in transgression." (Proverbs 29:22)

God does not want us to be angry. He knows how anger can get out of control and bad things can happen. When a person is angry he seems to forget what will happen if he acts while angry. People often get hurt, either physically, emotionally, or mentally.

June 28, 1914 in Sarajevo, Bosnia a young man named Gavrilo Princip shot and killed Archduke Ferdinand and his wife. This started World War I and eventually more than twenty countries became involved in the war. Millions of people died during the next four years.

Could anger have started this war? After the war many citizens were angry at people of other nations because of the death of their loved ones. Just as during the years of time, many innocent people have been killed, all because of other angry people wanting their own way.

When we do become angry at what we think is a wrong, we need to make peace with the other person.

"Be ye angry, and sin not: let not the sun go down upon your wrath (anger): Neither give place to the devil." (Ephesians 4:27)

Ephesians 4:31 tells us to put anger away from us. Don't let the devil win a victory in our lives. If we are angry with someone we should go to them and make peace as soon as possible!

Related Proverbs verses:14:17; 15:18; 16:32; 19:11,19

The Pure Word of God

Read: Proverbs 30

Verse: "Every word of God is pure: he is a shield unto them that put their trust in him. Add thou not unto his words, lest he reprove thee, and thou be found a liar." (Proverbs 30:5-6)

Agur wrote this chapter. We do not know who Agur was. He does not seem to think he is a very good man or knew God well. In verse three he says he did not learn wisdom, but he gave much good advice.

In verse five he says every word of God is pure. Verse six warns not to add to God's words. The word 'pure' means only what belongs in something is in it. Example, pure water only has water in it. There is no flavor, color, dirt, or anything else. It is only water. No one wants to drink or use dirty water.

The Word of God is pure. Every word in the Bible is pure. The Bible does not need to be changed or rewritten. It is a miracle of God that we have the same Word of God after these many years. The Word of God is the same yesterday, today, and forever

God warns that no person should add to or take away from God's word.

"For I testify unto every man that heareth the words of the prophecy of this book, If any man shall add unto these things, God shall add unto him the plagues that are written in this book: And if any man shall take away from the words of the book of this prophecy, God shall take away his part out of the book of life, and out of the holy city, and from the things which are written in this book. " (Revelation 22:18-19)

Today there are cults who try to pull people into false religions. We should be careful of false teachers and their literature. We should not permit people who teach false religions to come into our homes or accept their literature. We should be careful and keep the Word of God pure and clean.

Related Proverbs verses: 13:13; 19:16

Thought: God has kept the Bible pure for us today.

In Your Word I hope,
Dear God
For without Your Word
there is no hope.

A Virtuous Woman

Read: Proverbs Chapter 31

Verse: "Who can find a virtuous woman? for her price is far above rubies." (Proverbs 31:10)

> Julia Ward Howe and Anna Jarvis made the first known suggestion for a Mother's Day. Mother's Day received national recognition May 9, 1914. Children honor mothers with cards or gifts on this special day.

More than half of this chapter is about the virtuous (pure) woman who took care of her household duties with wisdom and understanding. She not only cared for her own family, but had concern for others. Fearing (trusting) God, she did things to honor Him.

"And whatsoever ye do, do it heartily, as to the Lord, and not unto men;" (Colossians. 3:23)

Maybe this woman seems unreal. She surely had times of weariness and struggles just as women do today, but did her work with a willing heart and mind for her family. She knew when things are done in order, other things are easier.

We should take care of our house and family to honor God. We could do things in a certain order. This order could be: 1: Time alone with God (Bible reading and prayer). 2: Husband. 3: Children; 4: Personal care. 5: Household duties; 6: Other activities. These items do not have to be in exact order. But, by keeping everything in balance, our family can honor us when our home is honoring to God.

Related Proverbs verses: 14:1; 18:22; 19:14; 31:10-31

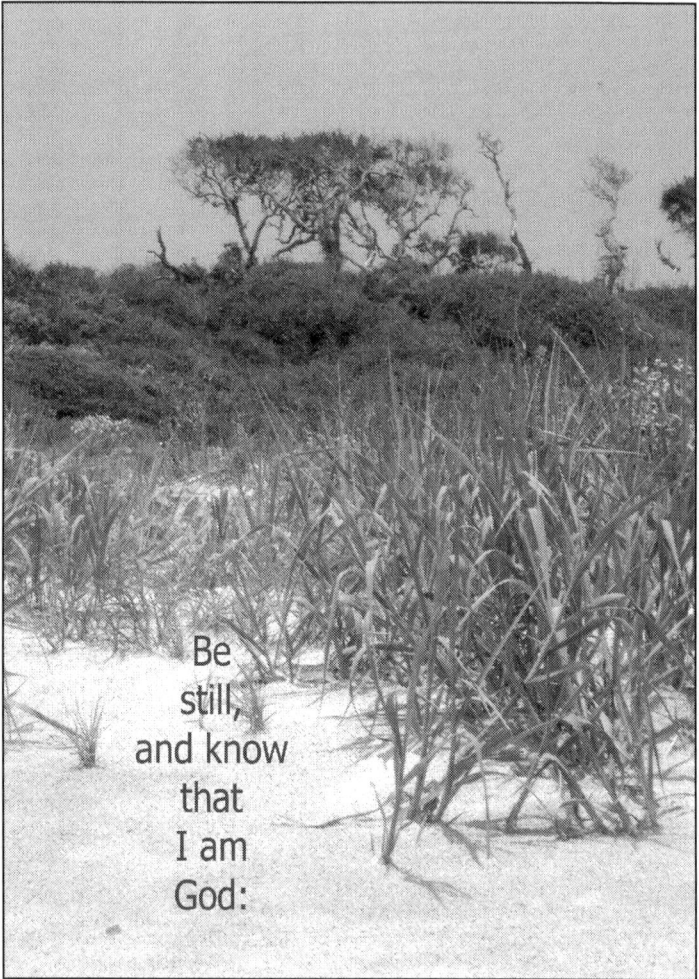

Be
still,
and know
that
I am
God:

Psalm 46:10

Made in the USA
Las Vegas, NV
05 November 2021

33676967R00030